# Plan The Life You Need

*"Shifting Oneself, Redefining Values, And Rethinking Priorities For The Life You Need."*

## Revitalize Your Best Self

Motsamai...
Keep Going

ISBN: 978-0-620-82426-2

**Written by:**
Coach Motsamai
+27 606539238

GLITZ PUBLISHERS

+27 606539238
info@glitzpublishers.com
www.glitzpublishers.com

# Table of Contents

# INTRODUCTION

Motsamai
Keep Going

Have you ever imagined living with an unshakable belief that you have what it takes to achieve anything you want, no matter what is happening around you? Imagine never feeling frightened by challenging circumstances, knowing that even if the worst happens, you can still pull yourself together, and do what is necessary to get your life back on track. Such imagination can be achieved if you believe in your ability to handle whatever comes your way; which is more effective than trying to guard against potential threats. *"Plan The Life You Need"* aims at shifting oneself, redefining values, and rethinking priorities for the life you need.

Most people plan for failure without knowing so, instead of pushing against the odds and breaking free. A pessimistic approach towards life only limits your potential. It is no lie that the only barrier to positive change is yourself; you are your enemy towards positive change.

At some point in life, you may be overwhelmed by lack, underachievement, and elementary living standards. There are lots of reasons as to why you fail to have a meaningful life. If you do not plan well, it's easy to make bad decisions. I encountered various challenges which harmed my social, economic, and academic aspirations.

I blamed my parents, the system, and mostly myself. I had a faulty perception because of a poor belief system. I never prioritized the things that could benefit my personal growth. I often saw myself as somewhat content with life the way things were. It is hard to think of anything else when real issues are identified and need your attention.

Nonetheless, I never quit but aspired for something deeper, and more meaningful. Looking back then I believe I denied myself the opportunity to be an ordinary human being. My perception about life was that "life sucks and not fair." I failed to understand that there are beautiful, sad, and ugly moments that will be beyond my control.

From such encounters, I realized I was not living the life I wanted. There came a time when I didn't need any more motivation. I realized that if you are not satisfied with where you stand in life now, don't expect that some inspirational quotes will change that. Yes, you can be motivated but the real change happens when you decide to plan strategically and take action on your ideas. Whenever you put your plans into action, shifting takes place.

The saddest truth about life is that you can't control everything. You are not the one holding the strings, God is. You can't have control over life, nobody can, except God. What you can do is make good use of the lessons life teaches you daily. Say you make a mistake, fail at something, experience heartbreak, or lose someone close to you; take these hiccups as valuable lessons. They are there to teach you the essence of life.

Nothing just happens in life. Sometimes you must wait more years to gain experience and learn a skill. You won't change the things you don't like about yourself until you decide to do so yourself. Proper planning, and revitalizing your best self are all needed to unleash your hidden potential. Things that you go through now will make sense later on in life.

As you go through this book, you will realize that change and becoming your best self is a process. Just so we are clear, this book is not about what doesn't kill you makes you stronger, because we know that most of the time what doesn't kill you devastates you mentally. You will come across the word "*success*" multiple times. Success, particularly in this book, means moving from point "A" to "B", "C" to "D", and so forth. As a life coach specializing in personal development, my goal is to help you revitalize your best self, and live the life you always wanted. *"Without hard work, nothing grows but weeds"*- Gordon. B. Hinckley.

# MEDIOCRE MENTALITY

*Motsamai...*
*Keep Going*

The choices we make can either make us live a meaningful life, or the worst life ever. Self-discipline plays a big role in our lives whenever we encounter challenges, limitations, and setbacks. What distinguishes us is how we respond to such conditions. To identify some of the reasons or rather, the habits that make you unable to fulfil your dreams and goals can be daunting. You need the ability to identify the root cause of the problems hindering you from achieving your goals. If I may ask, what is it that makes your life a living hell? What torments you?

Every path that leads to success is filled with obstacles. However, sometimes the biggest obstacles that keep you from achieving your goals could be obstacles of your own making. Nothing is more powerful than a positive mind. By the same token though, nothing can derail your progress towards achieving your goals as quickly as a negative mindset. Negative thoughts are like a bucket of water thrown on the fires of determination. Negative thoughts kill your determination and steal good ideas before they have a chance to develop. Similar to planning and setting goals, everyone wants to achieve their goals yet sadly, only a small percentage of people reach their goals in the end. What about you? Are you running your life, or does life run you?

Many people set their targets but fail to hit them. How about you? If you are like the majority; you set goals and fail to reach them, you need to find the reason why. To have a progressive life, you need to know why you consistently fail, then you can come up with a plan to overcome, and achieve what you need. For things to shift positively in your life, there has to be a shifting taking place with oneself first, then you can actualize shifting in other areas of your life.

Winners plan well and revitalize their best selves consistently. You too can restore your best self with a proper plan, to challenge your weaknesses and win. Failing to plan, leads to mediocrity. You don't want that, do you? People with mediocre mentality always have someone to blame, are good at making excuses, and don't want to take responsibility. Responsibility to them adds more pressure and torment.

*With that in mind, let's look into some of the weaknesses that are probably leading you to a mediocre mentality:*

## Poor Time Management

One of the reasons you fail to achieve what you want is that you don't create time for the things that matter most. You might have a passion for building a bigger house, starting a business, or growing a new income stream, but you don't have time to do it. You would like to spend 30 minutes reading, and another 30 minutes for exercise, but you just can't seem to find the extra time for these activities. If this is what describes you, you need to learn to prioritize the right things.

Create time, as there will always be enough time, if only you learn how to manage yourself, and choose to work on things that truly matter. Everyone has 24 hours a day, and no matter what you do, you cannot create more time. Therefore, it is all about how you manage yourself, your time, and your priority tasks.

## Lack of Knowledge

A lot of people say that they have no idea how to do something, but in fact, it is not that they don't know, they just refuse to use their brain to think. How do you lose weight? How do you build a business? How do you create a successful blog? How do you do marketing for your online business? You can find answers from other people who have done it before.

Like what Anthony Robbins said, "Success leaves clues." Everything that you ever wanted to accomplish, has already been accomplished by someone else out there. All you need to do is to find the answer on how it is done, or how they did it. Search on the internet, read books, and ask someone who has done it before.

## Inadequate Commitment

Are you 100% committed to achieving your goals? Are you willing to do whatever it takes to reach your goals? Or you will just do what is convenient? The thing is, you need to put in 100% commitment if you are serious about maximizing your potential. I have seen people who say that they want to build a business at night, but as soon as they reach home from work, they watch

TV instead. When you are committed, you will do whatever it takes wherein failure is never an option. You will sleep at 2 am, and get up at 5 am to work on your goals. Mediocre people are never committed to their goals, or pursue the life they want. They just say that they want, or they wish to reach their goals, but they are not committed.

I had to stop watching TV in the evenings. I quickly realized that I could be using that time for more writing, working on my business, or most importantly, spending time with my family. Soon after I made this change, my productivity improved, and was able to engage in more constructive activities. The quality of my life started to improve, and still, I felt like I could work much harder to achieve my goals.

## You Give Up Way Too Soon.

Do you know that success takes time? You cannot become an overnight success unless you win the lottery. A lot of people think that success is about doing that one thing, and they will be successful. No, it is not. Success is about doing consistent hard work throughout the day, every day! Most people give up when they don't see the results they expect. Some quit after a few months, a few weeks, and some quit just after a few days. Lionel Messi once said, "It took me 17 years and 114 days to be an overnight success."

Extraordinary people spend years before they manage to produce a remarkable result in their work. Do you think Michael Jordan, Steve Jobs, Bill Gates, and Warren Buffett achieved their outstanding success in a short period? Not at all. They have gone through many setbacks, failures, challenges, and hardships, but they never gave up. So, don't give up, rather, choose to work on revitalizing your best self. Remember the inspirational quote from Finding Dory? - "Just keep swimming." Always have the urge to keep moving up. Consistency is the key factor in mastering and actualizing your best self. Just don't ever quit on yourself.

## You Procrastinate, and Never Take Action.

The ultimate killer of your goals is not taking action only but also, procrastination. People tend to procrastinate because taking action can be challenging, difficult, and boring. If this is why you fail to reach your goals, you need to learn to build self-discipline. Create a daily routine, and stay consistent with it. People choose to follow their feelings and be controlled by their emotions throughout the day. They choose to sleep more because it feels good. If you are all about your feelings and emotions, you will procrastinate. You need to live your life with principles, not feelings.

Successful people have feelings too, yet they learn to manage their feelings and control their emotions better. That is why they take action regardless of whether they feel like it or not. They choose to wake up at 5 am, even if it is raining and they feel like continuing to sleep. They know that if they want to be successful, they need to live their life with principles, and not let their feelings control them.

## You Have a Fear of Success.

While the fear of failure is a clear reason why you avoid pursuing your goals, there is a fear that is often harder to recognize: the fear of success. Why would you be afraid of success? Well, there are several reasons:

Firstly, **Lack of Belief in Yourself**: If you don't truly believe in your ability to get (and stay) successful, you will avoid forward progress at all costs. You may subconsciously feel that even if others believe you to be successful, you still feel like a fraud. That would be an uncomfortable position to be in. So, you hold yourself back until you feel "ready" to be successful.

Secondly, **Fearing Increased Responsibility**: You might be resisting a higher level of achievement because you don't feel capable of handling all the responsibility that would inevitably come with it. Once you become successful, you will have certain obligations and steps that need to be taken to maintain your level of success. That can be frightening, and you may doubt your ability to handle the new challenges you will face.

Thirdly, **Low Self-Worth**: if you don't believe you deserve to be successful and happy, you will gravitate towards a position in life that matches your self-image. If you believe you deserve to be earning R1.5m per year, you will continue to do so. Trying to force yourself to increase your income will be futile because subconsciously you will resist it.

Fourthly, **Worries about What Others Will Think**: This goes along with low self-worth. You may have a habit of letting others define you rather than forging your path. You might believe that rich and successful people are dishonest, cruel, rude, cold, greedy, or any number of other stereotypes.

You may not have any identifiable fears about success, but rather experience a general sense of uneasiness or resistance to it. You might simply be afraid of the unknown, or pessimistic about the longevity of your success. Just remember that most fears relating to success are completely groundless. You fear the possibility of something happening, but such an occurrence is so remote that it's not even worth worrying about. Ninety-nine percent of the time we realize we were just being paranoid.

However, even with realistic fears that aren't so groundless, we are usually pleased and surprised to discover that we can work through any challenges that may arise. The realization of your fear ends up not being such a big deal after all. If you can't come up with a single uneasy feeling regarding your success, then it is possible that you simply don't have any fear of success. Not everyone does. Your sole obstacle might be staying disciplined, forming a solid plan, or even simply getting clear about what you want.

### You Never Improve After You Fail.

You can't reach your goals if you never improve after you have failed. One of the keys to creating extraordinary results in life is to learn and keep improving from the results you get in life.

If you try something and fail, then you should learn and improve, or do something else so that you will get different results. You will get the same old results if you refuse to change, and keep doing the same thing. When I say change, I mean changing your strategies, not your goals or your dreams.

Most people don't do this. When they fail, they think that they did not work hard enough. So, they pour more effort and time into it. Guess what, they will get the same result, just faster this time. So, dare to try something new, and do something different from time to time. Learn from your mistakes, and setbacks, and keep improving.

## Your Goals Are Vague.

Are your goals clear and specific? When you ask people what they want in their lives, most will give you vague answers such as they want to be rich, or they want to be happy. No wonder most people fail to reach their goals. The term "happy" is not clearly defined. How can you be happy? What makes you happy? Thus, there is no way you can tell if you have achieved it. The same goes if you say that your goal is to be rich. How much do you want? Is earning an additional R10k considered rich, or do you need to earn an additional R100k? You need to be clear and specific with what you want.

## You Listen To The Wrong Crowd.

There will be a lot of people who will tell you that your goals are impossible, or they are too difficult, or nobody has ever done it before. Some people will not tell you these, but they will tell you to get a job when your goal is to build a business. Well, what should you do? Just ignore the naysayers, and don't listen to them. When you have a dream or a goal, you have to protect it. Never let anyone tell you what you can or cannot do. Never let other people's opinions become your reality.

Choose to believe in yourself, and do what you think is right. Follow your heart, and chase your dreams. If you listen to people who say that it is impossible, or you should get a job in the graveyard/ cemetery because you failed in school, then you are living their expectations, not yours. Don't let other people define your life. You should be the one to choose how you want to live. So, ignore the naysayers.

# PLANNING THE LIFE YOU NEED

Motsamai
Keep Going

H ave you ever set goals and never achieved them, tried various strategies to deal with persistent challenges, or felt stuck and hopeless for positive change in your life? Well, planning the life you need, and revitalizing your best self, can help you to maximize your true potential against anything holding you back. Harriet Beecher Stowe once said that when you get into a tight place and everything goes against you, till it seems as though you cannot hold on a minute longer, she reckons that you should not give up, as that is just the place and time that your situation is about to change positively.

Before you can attain true healing, you must first recognize your wounds. This means that before you rebuild your sense of worth, you must first acknowledge how broken you are. If I may ask, where is your self-esteem founded? How firm is that foundation? Are you confident because you are good-looking? And what if you mingle among others who look better than you? And for how long will you stay that way? What happens when you grow older and that beauty fades away? Or, are you secure with your business success? What if the business or the reputation you've built suddenly falls? What are you worth by then?

For how long could you hold on to your riches? Can you still enjoy any of it as your body rots in the grave? All our efforts to increase our self-esteem are futile for, in the end, all such efforts lead only to fear, the fear of losing everything we have ever gained.

Life is based on forming positive relationships with other individuals or groups of people to function effectively, be it at home, school, workplace, and society in general. You cannot achieve your goals in isolation. In most instances, your problems surface due to inadequate positive relationships, and failing to manage such relationships. For you to be able to form positive relationships, it is important that you know the group you keep.

It is also critical to remember that how people relate to you, is based on your character which concludes their perception about you. Instead of worrying about how people perceive you, rather work on developing your character, as your character will determine their perception. This will, in turn, help build positive relationships as they will relate to you according to your genuine character. Les Brown, a world-known motivational speaker illustrated that life is beautiful, and sometimes it can get a little crazy, and feel out of control, or even too big to handle. He emphasized that it is in those moments that you need to sit back and remember what matters most, be it your sanity, health, or your ability to start over and discover your best self.

You could lose everything today, but you can never lose your ability to start over again. The most important aspect of planning the life you need is that you need to know and identify who you are not, so that you can determine who you are.

If you don't know who you are, the friends you keep will determine who you are, and should that happen, you have no control over yourself. Hence it is crucial that you revitalize your best self so that you can stand the test of time with more resilience.

**Let's look at the five steps that focus on creating, developing your life plan, the process of becoming your best self, and maintaining your personal growth, in the next chapters.**

# 1

# Outline Your Life Plan

*Motsamai*
*Keep Going*

We all have hopes, dreams, and aspirations in this life. But how many people achieve the goals they set? This is all on you, as you are the one to decide what your limits are, and the level of success you want. You are responsible for every decision you make. Oftentimes you spend a lot of time thinking or talking about what you want but, you never take action or steps to work on what you desire. It's not because you're lazy, but you don't have a well-defined life plan.

Life planning serves as a guide to making your dream a reality, helps you when your life feels out of control, and struggle to make decisions. A life plan is a reminder of what you want to achieve in life. It helps you realize your dreams, and meet your personal and professional goals. There's no reason why you can't achieve your goals when you have a well-defined plan.

Oftentimes that which holds you back is the fear of failure. A life plan can help you overcome this fear, and it doesn't have to be incredibly detailed, instead, it serves as a general guide and should be flexible because life is unpredictable. Your life plan should leave room for unforeseen possibilities, changes, and unpleasant circumstances.

Like any long and multi-faceted excursion, thoughtful planning is a key component of any successful life-learning. Some spontaneity in your learning is valuable, but to get the most out of your journey, it helps to do some planning, such as identifying your goals, understanding different ways to achieve them, listing the skills you will need, calculating how much it will cost, and planning for anticipated setbacks. It's also good to know how long the various legs of your journey will take. Similar to traveling on a **journey**; you need to outline your plan precisely, focusing on the **origin**, **destiny**, **vehicle**, **backpack**, **landmarks**, and **route**. With that been said, let's look into these critical considerations of a journey regarding planning the life you need:

### Find Your Origin

The Origin entails who you are. Your origin is who you are right now. For instance, most people when asked to introduce themselves, would say, "Hi, I'm Simon, 17 years old, and a senior student at school." It does not tell who Simon is, but it only tells you his present preoccupation. To gain insights about yourself, you need to look closely at your beliefs, values, and principles aside from your economic, professional, cultural, and civil status.

Moreover, you can also reflect on your experiences to give you insights on your good, and not-so-good traits, skills, knowledge, strengths, and weaknesses. Locate your origin, it all starts within, by understanding your standpoint in life.

## Identify Your Destination

The destination is a vision of who you want to be. Who do you want to be? It is important that you know yourself, to have a clear idea of who you want to be, and the things you want to change, whether they are attitudes, habits, or points of view. If you hardly know yourself, then your vision and goals for the future will also be unclear. Your destination should cover all the aspects of your being: the physical, emotional, intellectual, and spiritual.

## Getting a Proper Vehicle

A vehicle is what you use to reach your destination. It can be analogized to your mission or vocation in life. To a great extent, your mission depends on what you know about yourself. You may decide that you want to become a medical doctor, therefore, your life mission is to live a life dedicated to serving your fellowmen as a medical doctor in conflict areas.

## Preparing Your Travel Bag

The travel bag is similar to your knowledge, skills, and attitude. Food, drinks, medicines, and other traveling necessities are contained in a bag. Applying this concept to your life map, you also bring with you certain knowledge, skills, and attitudes. These determine your competence and can help you reach your vision. Given such, there is a need for you to assess what knowledge, skills, and attitudes you have at present, and what you need to gain along the way.

## Setting Identifiable Landmarks

Landmarks confirm if you are on the right track while the route determines the travel time. In planning out your life, you also need to have landmarks and a route. These landmarks are your measures of success. These measures must be specific, measurable, attainable, realistic, and time-bound. Thus, you cannot set two major landmarks such as earning a master's degree and a doctorate within a period of two years since the minimum number of years to complete a master's degree is two years.

Going back to the mission of becoming a medical doctor, landmarks in your life map will be completing a bachelor's degree in biology by the age of 21; completing medicine by the age of 27; earning your specialization in infectious diseases by the age of 30; getting deployed in local public hospitals of your town by the age of 32; and serving as a doctor in war-torn areas by the age of 35.

## Always Anticipate Turns, Detours, and Potholes.

The purpose of your life map is also to minimize hasty and spur-of-the-moment decisions that can make you lose your way. But oftentimes our plans are modified along the way due to some inconveniences, delays, and other situations beyond our control. Like in any path, there are turns, detours, and potholes, which you must anticipate and adjust accordingly.

# Tips To Keep in Mind as You Create Your Life Plan

## Be Honest About What You Want, And Who You Want to Become

Remember, it's your life-learning journey. Your dreams and aspirations are the foundation of this trip. They should frame your decisions about what you study, the experiences you want to engage in, and the destinations where your activities will lead. Own the process. It's okay to get feedback on your journey, but don't let someone else's goals for you dictate your path.

## Be Clear About Where You Want to Go

It's almost impossible to arrive someplace specific without identifying clearly where that someplace is. After spending time reflecting on your dreams and aspirations, you should be ready to start defining your journey's destination(s), as well as the goals you want to meet along the way.

## Know Where You Are Now Before Heading Out

At one time or another, most of us have stood in front of a big map trying to figure out where we are, concerning where we want to go. Most of these maps are marked with a big "X" and the words, "You are here!" The starting point is marked clearly for one simple reason: it's impossible to get where we want to go if we don't know where we are. It's the same when navigating your life-learning journey. Knowing where you are starting from gives you a location from which you can plan the best routes to arrive at your planned destination. It also helps you measure the distance you have travelled and how much farther you have before you reach your next goal. Knowing your starting point for your life-learning journey includes an honest assessment of your current knowledge, skills, and experiences. What do you already know? What can you already do? Where are the gaps in your knowledge?

## Know Your Exits Well

Not surprisingly, not every journey goes as planned. There are unexpected opportunities, personal interruptions, and other "life got in the way" interludes. You should expect these and realize, from the outset, that your journey will require you to make unplanned stops. For this reason, it's a good idea to know where you can exit conveniently with as little lost effort or momentum as possible. Finding and planning proactively to use timely exit ramps will keep you moving forward efficiently on your journey and excited about the progress you have made.

## Keep Your Life Plan Readily Available

When you see your goals, dreams, and plans repeatedly, you are more likely to keep them in mind whenever you make a decision. Whether you write your life plan on paper or create one online, make sure your plan is visible to you daily (e.g., taped to your bathroom mirror, saved on to your desktop, etc.)

## Have Someone to Hold You Accountable

Adhering to life plans becomes easier when you allocate someone to check in on your progress. Whether it's your partner, a friend, or a life coach, ask someone you trust to gently discuss your goals with you every few days (or weeks or months). Knowing that you have someone to report to or update will help increase your consistency towards achieving your goals.

## Do Your Best to Be Flexible

Life may throw you curveballs before you even pick up the bat. When changes arise that may affect your plans, it may help to be open about changing your objectives, amending your priorities, and reviewing your life plan to adjust it as you see fit.

# 2

# KNOW YOUR GOALS INSIDE OUT

*Motsamai...*
*Keep Going*

G oals are similar to the mission statements or mandates of your plan. To master your goals, you need to list all the goals that you have identified. If you are not certain of what you want in life, you are just bound to receive the unexpected. Verily though, goals should always be sensible and accomplishable. Setting unrealistic goals is of no use. Writing down your goals helps you to outline your priorities. You need to start by writing the important goals at the top of the list and number them accordingly.

Knowing your goals inside out gives hope, and enables you to identify blind spots. Blind spots that you need to take into consideration could be related to comparison, poor belief systems, low self-esteem, poor time management, and investing in the wrong systems and schemes of life.

Once you know your goals inside out, you will have a clear sense of direction and purpose, and provide you with a platform to revitalize your best self.

Remember, a person who has managed to revitalize their best self, can unlock his or her hidden potential, and maximize their strengths.

## WAYS YOU CAN USE TO MASTER YOUR GOALS INSIDE OUT:

### Develop a Strategy

Once you have listed your goals, you need to evaluate and develop a strategy to reach your goals. For example, if your goal is to shed some extra weight, your broad strategy should be dieting and exercise. Nothing can be achieved straightforwardly in life. So, you need a particular strategy and dedication to pull off your goals.

### Have Definite Action Plans

Once your broad line of attack is determined, work on your definite action plans. For instance, if dieting and exercising are your broad strategies for your weight loss goal, then your action plan should consist of a healthy diet chart; a healthy way of life, and an appropriate workout routine.

### Believe In Yourself

If you want to accomplish your goals and become successful in life, you have to believe in yourself. All successful men and women today are doing well because they believe in themselves, and are confident about their capabilities. If you believe in yourself, then you can accomplish the goals you have set for yourself.

## Review Your Progress

Make sure you are making progress. Review your progress every week to analyze how far you have reached in accomplishing your goals. If you find that you are lagging, hire a coach, look for help from family and friends, and above all, try to recognize why your goal is not being met. Find a solution to accomplish your goal. Maybe you looked at this list and realized you hadn't visited your parents in a while, didn't take a vacation last year, or missed participating in a hobby that you loved.

Once you have made a list of your top priorities, you may find it helpful to create some goals that can help you increase your satisfaction with these different life aspects. Oftentimes, psychologists and other professionals may recommend making SMART goals for yourself. If the term "SMART goals" is unfamiliar to you, here is a brief overview of what a SMART goal can look like.

**Specific:** Specific goals are clear and often focused. For example, if you want to cultivate more intentional time with your partner, a specific goal could be to spend alone time with your partner every week.

**Measurable:** Measurable Goals have an aspect that you can quantify to see whether you are progressing toward your goal.

Perhaps you and your partner decide you want to take 2 hours of your time every Friday for a date night.

**Attainable:** You likely want to ensure that you are capable of accomplishing this goal. This could include making the goal more achievable and listing out alternatives for when changes happen or crises arise. Maybe you ask a sibling or parent to take care of your kids every Friday for a couple of hours so you and your partner can go on this date night.

**Relevant:** Relevant Goals will be grounded in your core values and priorities. Let's say you have been feeling disconnected from your partner. If you are seeking more fulfillment in the romance or marriage department, spending more time with your partner may be a relevant goal for you.

**Time-Bound**: Successful SMART goals have deadlines that can help you stay motivated in reaching your goals. Let's assume you have an anniversary trip coming up in a couple of months, and you want to rekindle the romance with your partner before the trip. You may plan to have five date nights until that trip to feel reconnected with your partner.

## Also, Set Mindset Goals.

Having the right mindset is critical. The correct mindset is needed to win over challenging circumstances. A proper mindset helps you achieve your goals. As you look at your goals for the year, quarter, or week, ask yourself what mindset is required to help you succeed. Are your goals oriented around growth and personal development? If so, self-acknowledgement, gratitude, and grace might be appropriate mindsets.

If your big goal is to start a new company or launch a new project, relevant values might be focus, patience, and grit. Make sure you start with and stay in the right mindset to help you achieve your goals. Set mindset goals to help you stay in the zone and focus on your big goals.

## How Does One Go About Setting Mindset Goals?

### Align Your Goals with Your Values

Many people set goals in a vacuum that can seem arbitrary in hindsight – generate R10M in revenue, change jobs, or get a promotion. Go further and align your goals with your values. For people with a clear, established purpose and values, ask yourself if your goals line up with your values. For me, I have strong, enduring values of growth (both personally and professionally, though it's increasingly the same), freedom of time and space, and family.

Rather than just set a revenue target for the year (which I do), I also focus on goals that help me live out my values; serving clients that allow me to grow professionally, minimizing travel so that I can be there for my family, and not overscheduling my days so that I can continue to write, create, and grow.

Aligning my values and goals provides more meaning in my days, weeks, and months, while giving me a greater chance of achieving my goals. If you have yet to set a clear set of values, ask yourself "why" a particular goal matters to you. Is it rooted in ego, greed, or recognition (which is fine by the way if that is important to you)? Or is it anchored in meaning? This time around set goals that align with your values and what matters most to you.

## Set both "Being" and "Achieving" Goals

Most peoples' goals are rooted in achievement or attainment; make R200K, buy a new house, or write a book. To help you achieve those goals, also set "being" goals. For me, it's a greater focus on being patient, accepting where I am in my career and life, and being present each day. What about you? Are you solely focused on achievement and attainment? Try a greater focus on "being" this time and see if you are both more successful in achieving your goals, but also experience more joy, calm, and satisfaction along the way.

## Focus on the Process, Not Just the Outcomes

Goals are intended to be achieved. But goals are like a scoreboard that doesn't always tilt in your favor. Be sure to focus on the process, and not just the outcomes as much progress can be made even if you fall short of your goals. Perhaps you are trying to be a better leader with your team and aim to be more present in one-on-one team meetings.

Don't solely focus on the rewards of being more present in meetings. Acknowledge the fact that you are taking 5 minutes before each meeting to center yourself and get ready to show up for the other person. Focusing on and rewarding the process will help prevent frustration when goals take longer than expected to achieve. They will also shift your mind to what you can control (the process) versus what you cannot (the outcome).

## Acknowledge Your Progress

Effective goals are those that are achievable but also aspirational. For goals that require you to take risks, shift into a state of discomfort, and experience fear, be sure to acknowledge your progress along the way. Acknowledge that you just asked a long-standing client for a referral rather than solely rewarding the successful outcome. Doing hard things requires self-acknowledgement because external validation can take time or be hard to come by.

## Flush Goals that Don't Serve You

I don't know about you, but certain goals sit on my goals sheet year after year but are never achieved. Why that is true for me and so many others? Many are those that don't align with core values. Others might just not be motivated anymore. Have the courage to flush goals on your list that no longer serve or motivate you. Seeing goals that are never achieved acts as a drag on motivation and confidence to achieve the other goals on the list. Go ahead and flush that goal that no longer serves or motivates you.

# 3

# PLACE YOURSELF AT THE RISK OF OPPORTUNITIES

*Motsamai* 🦶🦶
*Keep Going*

Placing yourself at the risk of opportunities is about actualizing your plan, maintaining positive personal growth, taking action toward opportunities, networking, and asking the right questions. Successful people are always vulnerable to opportunities as they develop a routine that helps them maximize their potential, and lead a positive life instead of surviving life. If you think that opportunities will just fall into your lap, then you are in for a big surprise. You need to pop off that couch and find ways to attract opportunities to your life.

This isn't a hippie suggestion where I tell you to open up your window to bring down the positive energy of the universe (though it wouldn't hurt, right?) Rather, there are certain good habits that you can fall into, and make them part of your daily routine which can get your name out there, make people aware of you, and live life at your best. The more places your name floats around, then the more people are aware you exist, which leads to more opportunities being thrown your way. It's really simple but a lot of people fail to do it — all it takes is making sure you put yourself out there. Granted that might take more work than you're putting in now, but like I mentioned before, good things don't usually just fall into laps!

If you keep yourself developing, progressing with skills, sharing accomplishments with your industry, and giving as many good vibes back as you receive, you'll be on your way to living your life fulfilled. *To learn how you can place yourself at the risk of opportunities, you need to at least consider the following aspects:*

### Ask the Right Questions

Needing to ask questions places you at the doorstep of opportunities, and it becomes more effective if you ask information-seeking questions. Curiosity will push you to ask questions. When you wake up in the morning, think about the things you would like to do that day.

Instead of diving into very deep thoughts, ask yourself constructive questions that could help solve a particular problem. If you are not able to answer your questions, seek help, and ask the right questions from various sources. You should prepare your daily routine every morning, to perform your tasks on time. Try to plan it thoroughly, and whenever you achieve it, you will feel fulfilled and happy about yourself. Be strategic, no matter how unnecessary the subject might be. This way you will be prepared and less likely to feel stressed or anxious about the unknown.

### Learn to Prepare Earlier

If you can do something today, don't leave it for tomorrow. Entrepreneurs are individuals who are always at risk of opportunities in everything they do. Challenges to them are a source of opportunities. They know that through challenges, there is a valuable lesson and an income-generating opportunity. Creating an entrepreneurial mindset can place you at a good level of living the life you want. Have a grand vision, carefully considering all that you want in life, and imparting your dreams and principles into the right perspectives.

You need to ask yourself meaningful questions so that you can focus on more than just the day-to-day errands. The entrepreneur's mindset is useful in every aspect of your life. This way of thinking can be used to improve your relationships with your family, how you develop your hobbies and interests, and your parenting skills. Entrepreneurs are flexible and able learners. There is almost nothing in this life that they cannot do, more if there is a passion behind their hustle.

### Prepare for Future Opportunities

Unique personal opportunities for career and personal advancement, in fields that we are interested in, are all around us. Sometimes they don't manifest as quickly as we would like. However, we shouldn't get discouraged because there are some very specific things that we can do to prepare ourselves for future opportunities, and when they manifest, because of our preparation, we will be ready to provide significant value. Below I have listed *tips* that you must follow to prepare for opportunities ahead; even if you aren't working on your dream job or business right now, but if you do these things, opportunities will come into your life.

## Stay Informed About Developments

You should stay informed about what's going on in your field. What are the trends? Where are the opportunities right now? In a year? In five years? Developments will inform your education and networking efforts. However, if you aren't aware of what is going on, then you may miss out on opportunities that will manifest for those people who are in the right place at the right time. You can be that person by staying apprised of what is going on in the industry, and the world around you.

## Build Your Portfolio

There are things that we can do right now in our chosen fields to build our platform or portfolio, even if we think we aren't working in our ideal setting. Start a blog and create a meaningful contribution to the advancement of your field. Get involved with organizations, and research any volunteer or mentoring opportunities. The more you do, the more opportunities come your way.

## Make Learning a Habit

Embrace the opportunity that you have right now to educate yourself. Make learning a habit. Schedule time for it daily, and stick to your plan. How badly you want this opportunity will determine the priority that you place on your self-directed education. Do you want it bad enough to forsake your regular scheduled TV session tonight? The more you learn, the better prepared you will be to immediately contribute when you have the chance.

## Establish Positive Relationships with People

Network, network, network, but do it intelligently. Look to add value to people. Find ways that you can be a benefit to those whom you are looking to associate with. People always make time for those who can add value to their life. Be one of those types of people. This is where having some form of positive contribution (like writing or blogging) can be a significant entry into a new relationship. You can't attract new opportunities your way if those opportunities don't know where to knock. You need to get yourself out there and let people know you exist! And the best way to do that is to network.

Networking can open opportunities for career advancement. Not only should you network with people but, also network with people outside of your field. You never know what you may learn by networking with people of different occupations and trades. If you hate the idea of eating snacks and talking to strangers at an event, you can always network in other ways. Get close to industry people you admire or think are influential on Twitter, Instagram, TikTok, or Facebook, and you can always get in-depth conversations via online messaging. If they know about you, they'll send opportunities your way.

## Determine How You Are Going to Create Value

Ask yourself this question:  how I am going to create real value for others?  Take time to answer this question thoroughly.  Make a plan to create value, and then begin at once to execute your plan.  The more value that you can create for others, the more successful you will be, and the more opportunities will come your way.

## Place Yourselves Where Your Heart Wants to Be

You should consistently show up, that is, place yourself where your heart wants to be.  You say you want to become a writer, well, where is your writing?  Where is your book?  Where is your blog?  You don't need someone's permission to write; you simply need to start writing.  You say you want to be a business person?  Well, where is your business?   You don't need someone's permission to start a business; you just have to start one.

Are you interested in working in finance, public relations, healthcare, or a particular industry sector? Then, are you attending the important conferences and networking events in these areas? Have you received the education that you need to contribute value in these areas? If not, why not?

If you truly want something, you will place yourself where your heart wants to be.

## Say Goodbye to That Comfort Zone

If you stay where it's always cozy and nice, you've got no chance to grow! By stepping outside of your comfort zone you're giving yourself the chance to meet new people and land in new situations. The aim is to create opportunities by stepping outside the comfort zone instead of waiting for them. Otherwise, your life will be nothing more than comfortable. Are you not in the mood to go to that networking event? Grab your name badge and go. Are you too nervous to do that book reading? All the more reason to head out the door. Will you feel awkward going to a seminar or class alone? Just think of what might be waiting for you there!

## Share What You've Got

Are you an amazing writer? Then you better be producing articles or blog posts of some kind. Do you have an eye for style? Share your fashion tips with blogs or tutorials. Are you amazing at graphic design? Share some of your coolest tips and tricks. The more information you put out there, the more people will recognize your name and think of you as an expert. Create videos, power points, e-books, or even write a blog and give them away for free to other people in your industry! When you give back to others in the form of knowledge, you are also giving back to yourself by establishing yourself as an expert in your field.

By establishing yourself as a person who knows what they're about, your chances for getting opportunities and offers will increase. Want good vibes thrown your way? First, send some out yourself. Everyone out there is looking for opportunities and recognition, so help contribute. Whether you loved someone's article and tweeted your praise, were impressed with a project and emailed your love, or covered their genius in a blog post, building people up will make them take notice of you and possibly do the same back. If you have a colleague who works as hard as you, then praise that person...Be specific and sincere about what the person is doing. You never know what that kind of love can bring you. Nothing negative.

### See What Areas You Can Improve

The more developed, well-rounded, and newly-ambitious you are, the more opportunities you can nab. So, to make sure you're not stagnant or slowing down in your self-development, check in with your progress every month and see where you can pump up the energy. The key is to do monthly or quarterly self-reflection activities to evaluate your progress and analyze new areas requiring development. It is important to be systematic in your actions, as they will increase your chances in the long term to attract plenty of new opportunities, upwards and onwards!

### Speak to a Coach

Not only will you have someone to learn from, but you'll have someone you're close with, that could vouch for your hard-working nature and your smarts.

Life coaches offer valuable advice. The chances are that they have been through the same situations that you're experiencing, and can help you navigate them successfully. Also, if they're your mentor, chances are they're higher up in the industry than you, and you never know what kind of people they can introduce you to.

# 4

## CHANGE YOUR HABITS

Motsamai

Keep Going

As a man was passing the elephants, he suddenly stopped, confused by the fact that these huge creatures were being held by only a small rope tied to their front leg. No chains, no cages. It was obvious that the elephants could, at any time break away from their bonds but for some reason, they did not. He saw a trainer nearby and asked why these animals just stood there and made no attempt to get away.

"Well," the trainer said, "when they are very young and much smaller, we use the same size rope to tie them and, at that age, it's enough to hold them. As they grow up, they are conditioned to believe they cannot break away. They believe the rope can still hold them, so they never try to break free." The man was amazed. These animals could at any time break free from their bonds but because they believed they couldn't, they were stuck right where they were.

Like the elephants, how many of us go through life hanging onto a belief that we cannot do something, simply because we failed at it once before? Failure is a part of learning. We should never give up the struggle in life. You fail not because you are destined to fail, but because there are lessons that you need to learn as you move on with your life, and do away with bad habits. Bad habits can be a tricky thing. Everyone has them, but few have the self-awareness to identify them. Fewer still have what it takes to banish them and once you banish them, you can move forward faster. *Let's look at the few tips for not only busting bad habits but replacing them with successful habits:*

## Identify Bad Habits

As you might have guessed, the first step to eradicating bad habits is identifying them so you can weed them out. This can be easier said than done, as many of us tend to be in a state of denial about our bad habits, but as the saying goes, "Once you see the mess, you can clean up the mess." So, go ahead and take an inventory of the habits you currently have. I'm talking about ALL of them, good, bad, and in-between. Can you easily see the ones that are holding you back? Take the time to dive deep and be honest with yourself about the bad habits that are holding you back, be it checking social media too much, being lazy, or waking up late all the time.

## Figure Out the Underlying Cause

Once you've identified your bad habits, it's important to dig a little deeper to figure out the underlying cause. Say for instance that you procrastinate a lot. That's undeniably a bad habit, but simply recognizing that isn't going to stop it. It's recognizing what causes you to procrastinate that will help you make progress.

With procrastination, a common cause is fear of rejection or failure. You're scared that when you complete something, it will be found lacking or not good enough. Therefore, you put off finishing it because that puts off the rejection or negative feedback that scares you. By learning how to develop coping mechanisms for rejection or dealing with failure, you'll be able to banish that bad habit.

## Know the Triggers

In addition to figuring out the underlying cause, it's helpful to know what triggers your bad behaviour. For example, are you more likely to fall back into old habits when you haven't had enough sleep, or haven't eaten adequately? Or do you tend to make bad choices after you've argued with a loved one? Knowing what can trigger bad habits can help you avoid them. For example, if you know that you never have a productive day if you haven't eaten in the morning, for crying out loud, make it a point to wake up earlier and eat breakfast. Sometimes, little things like this can make an enormous difference.

## Choose a Habit to Put in Its Place

When you banish a bad habit, you'll be surprised how much space is left in its absence. To discourage another equally bad habit from forming in its place, make a conscious decision to replace it with a good habit. For example, say you have a bad habit of wasting time on social media. You've identified that it's a bad habit. You're aware that you indulge when you're bored and you've taken the proactive step of setting a timer and devoting a smaller amount of time to your social media binge time. This is great, but what are you going to do with the time you were wasting? Establishing a new habit, like reading the financial pages, browsing the world news, or reading people's success stories can help you fill in that void constructively so that you're not just losing a bad habit but building a good one.

## Know Your Purpose

Are you wandering through life with little direction - hoping that you'll find happiness, good health, and prosperity? Identify your life purpose or mission statement and you will have your unique compass that will lead you to your truth north every time. This may seem tricky at first when you see yourself to be in a tight or even a dead end. But there's always that little loophole to turn things around and you can make a big difference to yourself.

## Know Your Values

What do you value most? Make a list of your top 5 values. Some examples are security, freedom, family, spiritual development, and learning. As you set your goals for future reference - check your goals against your values. If the goal doesn't align with any of your top five values - you may want to reconsider it or revise it. The number shouldn't discourage you, instead, it should motivate you to do more than you can ever dream of.

## Know Your Needs

Unmet needs can keep you from living authentically. Take care of yourself. Do you have a need to be acknowledged, to be right, to be in control, to be loved? Many people live their lives without realizing their dreams, and most of them end up being depressed for that matter. List your top four needs and get them met before it's too late!

## Live From the Inside Out

Increase your awareness of your inner wisdom by regularly reflecting in silence. Commune with nature. Breathe deeply to quiet your distracted mind. For most of us, it's hard to find the peace we want even in our own homes. In my case, I often just sit in a dimly lit room and play some classical music. There's sound, yes, but music does soothe the savage beast.

## Start Your Day with Positive Affirmations

How you start the morning sets the tone for the rest of the day. Have you ever woken up late, panicked, and then felt like nothing good happened the rest of the day? This is likely because you started the day with a negative emotion and a pessimistic view that carried into every other event you experienced. Instead of letting this dominate you, start your day with positive affirmations. Talk to yourself in the mirror, even if you feel silly, with statements like, "Today will be a good day" or "I'm going to be awesome today." You'll be amazed by how much your day improves. Tell yourself positive things every day.

## Focus On the Good Things, However Small

Almost invariably, you're going to encounter obstacles throughout the day, there's no such thing as a perfect day. When you encounter such a challenge, focus on the benefits, no matter how slight or unimportant they seem. For example, if you get stuck in traffic, think about how you now have time to listen to the rest of your favourite podcast. If the store is out of the food you want to prepare, think about the thrill of trying something new. Find your silver lining.

## Find Humour in Bad Situations

Allow yourself to experience humour in even the darkest or most trying situations. Remind yourself that this situation will probably make for a good story later and try to crack a joke about it.

## Turn Failures into Lessons

You aren't perfect. You're going to make mistakes and experience failure in multiple contexts, at multiple jobs, and with multiple people. Instead of focusing on how you failed, think about what you're going to do next time—turn your failure into a lesson. Conceptualize this in concrete rules. For example, you could come up with three new rules for managing projects as a result. You're going to fail. Learn to use it to your advantage.

## Focus On the Present

I'm talking about the present—not today, not this hour, only this exact moment. You might be getting chewed out by your boss, but what in this exact moment is happening that's so bad? Forget the comment he made five minutes ago. Forget what he might say five minutes from now. Focus on this one, individual moment. In most situations, you'll find it's not as bad as you imagine it to be. Most sources of negativity stem from a memory of a recent event or the exaggerated imagination of a potential future event. Stay in the present moment. Be right where you are. Live at the moment.

## Find Positive Friends, Mentors and Co-Workers

When you surround yourself with positive people, you'll hear positive outlooks, stories, and affirmations. Their positive words will sink in and affect your line of thinking, which then affects your words and similarly contributes to the group. Finding positive people to fill up your life can be difficult, but you need to eliminate the negativity in your life before it consumes you. Do what you can to improve the positivity of others, and let their positivity affect you the same way. Surround yourself with these amazing people.

Almost anybody in any situation can apply these lessons to their own lives and increase their positive attitude. As you might imagine, positive thinking offers compound returns, so the more often you practice it, the greater the benefits you'll realize.

## Maintain Some Confidence

Confidence is certainly the most important factor that adds to the personality of any individual. A person's confidence might go down due to mistakes, failure, guilt, or any other undesirable thing. Some people often develop an inferiority complex due to their physical appearance, caste, financial status, etc. Such people perceive confidence as their weakness, while the truth is that confidence is an individual's biggest strength. Your confidence reflects your character, attitude, and passion.

## Know What Is Important in Your Life

What is important in your life? It will take time and effort. It might be easy for some of you but the hardest thing for most. Most will get stuck but then they will give more generic answers like more money, more time, etc. But when you ask them to dig deeper and find the real answers, they will feel uncomfortable.

# 5

# LIVE UP TO YOUR TRUE POTENTIAL

*Motsamai*
*Keep Going*

## Finding Balance and Meaning

If you allow other elements of your life to be negatively affected by your work, you won't be as mentally sharp and focused to do your best work, and you won't even be eager to return to the work you need to complete. For instance, if you are an entrepreneur working on a computer or mobile device to create products, and sell to people online, or if you are constantly working on your computer and never take breaks away from them to do other things, several areas of your life are going to suffer.

For one thing, your weight is probably going to increase, causing a detrimental effect on your health. That is because you are constantly sitting, looking at a screen, and typing away with your fingers, but that is about the only physical activity you'll be getting. If you do this hour-for-hour, day-by-day, week-by-week, over time, the food you are eating is likely going to go onto your frame as fat because you aren't doing enough physical activity to burn it off. As a result, your weight is going to increase and you will probably have a negative view of yourself when you look in the mirror or are around family or friends who may look at you differently because of your changed appearance. This is not going to help your mindset, and your mood when it comes to your work, which will negatively impact the quality of it and might even lead you to avoid the work altogether which will negatively impact your reputation, credibility, or business profitability.

Therefore, you need to take time out for yourself to work off the food you eat and stay in good, physical shape. Not only will this keep you in good physical health, but it will put you in a good mental state of mind too to where you can stay mentally focused and engaged in your work and do higher-quality work. It's not just your weight that will be negatively affected. Your social life will be negatively affected as well. If you have a family—spouse or even spouse and kids–they will not like the fact that they don't see you that often because you are constantly working.

Chances are you will drift farther apart from your spouse because you spend no quality time together. This will also happen with your kids as well, which could cause them to resent you because you spend no quality time with them. If your family starts to resent you not being there constantly, chances are high that the environment will be strained and you will constantly have that resentment and strain in the back of your mind, which will lead to you losing focus on your work, negatively impacting the quality of it. This is why it is critical that you set enough time in your schedule so that you can spend time with your family and loved ones, so that they know you still care for them even when you are busy with work. In addition to that, the break away from work will do you good as well, as your mind will get that much-needed time away from work so that you can be more mentally focused and engaged on the tasks you need to do to complete your projects.

Even if you are unmarried and don't have a family, it still will negatively impact you if you don't take breaks away from your work and head outside from time to time. If you cut yourself off from your friends, family members, or boyfriend/girlfriend, your mind will start to lose focus, and you will forget what it means to do anything other than work, which will negatively impact your social life and skills. Having a dull social life is not going to enrich your life any, especially since constantly working can cause your mind to become disinterested in your work and even cause you to resent your work.

This is all the more reason why you cannot afford to procrastinate and make excuses for why you are not getting tasks completed as quickly as you should; it's more than just actually completing the project, but managing the aspects of your life away from the projects you're working on—including family, friends/social life, diet, exercise, and more—to ensure you are in the best condition possible to do the best work possible.

Sometimes, when you feel like the world is just too heavy, look around and you will find people who continue to live fascinating and wonderful lives. How does one become genuinely happy with themselves?

## Learn to Love Yourself

To love oneself means to accept that you are not a perfect being but behind the imperfections, lie a great ounce of courage to be able to discover ways how to improve your repertoire to recover from your mistakes. Genuine happiness also pertains to contentment. When you are contented with the job you have, the way you look, with your family, your friends, the place you live in, your car, and all the things you now have–truly, you know the answer to the question "how to be genuinely happy?"

When you discover a small start somewhere from within, that small start will eventually lead to something else and do something else. But if you keep questioning life little it has never done you any good, you will never be able to find genuine happiness. I believe that life is about finding out about right and wrong, trying and failing, winning and losing. These are the things that happen as often as you inhale and exhale.

Show yourself constant self-love. This means putting yourself first. Permit yourself to prioritize your own need for rest, relaxation, exercise, and recuperation. By putting yourself first, you aren't being selfish – but rather – the opposite. Everyone in your life benefits when you take the time to reset and recharge. Self-love also means accepting you aren't perfect – and letting go of the notion everything needs to be just that.

There is beauty in imperfections. Identify the things in your life that give you energy – and prioritize those. Be sure to design a weekly routine to include these – don't let an unbalanced life in chaos gobble up the very things that put you in balance and help you eliminate that chaos.

## Do not Chase after Money

Just as happiness is not about money, neither is success about money. Don't choose your passion because of the money it can bring you. Don't overwork and exhaust yourself to earn more money. Don't focus on what you stand to gain from sharing your passion with the world. Such requests may sound counterproductive since abundant financial rewards are undoubtedly one indication of success.

Money does not guarantee success but is rather a side-effect of success. The reason I don't want you to focus on the money angle is that it will dilute your focus. You begin worrying about what you will "get" rather than what you can contribute to others. That might not seem like a big deal, but it is. There is an old saying that everything you do is infused with your energy.

We might clarify that to say everything you do is infused with the quality of your energy. Think about this for a moment and you'll realize the truth of such a statement. Have you ever done a task out of sheer obligation but your heart wasn't in it? Perhaps you wrote a report for school, completed a project at work, or even attended an event because your partner wanted to go but you had zero interest in it? What happened with those activities?

The report or project was likely passable as far as quality goes, but it probably didn't have any "oomph" did it?

And what of the event you attend for someone else's benefit? You probably spent the majority of the time bored out of your mind and didn't take anything valuable away from the experience. There's a good reason for this: you did not put forth high-quality energy, so you ended up with lukewarm results. And the same thing will happen with your level of success! You might be thinking, "Great! If I put a lot of energy into the thought of money, I'll get a lot of money back!" Actually no! It's not about the specific thoughts you are thinking, but the quality of energy you are putting out.

If you focus on what you stand to gain, you are detracting from what you plan to give. That means that you are not putting anything of value out there into the world, and you will, therefore, experience ineffective results with whatever you do. Ask yourself why successful people all seem to love what they do for a living, and you'll be moving in the right direction!

When you are at work, do you get frustrated because things don't seem to be happening the way they're supposed to be? You see people milling around but nothing gets accomplished. And in the daily hustle and bustle, do you feel that your goals remain just that, goals? Then maybe it's time for you to stand up and do something about it. Most people are content just to stand around listening and waiting for orders. And it isn't unusual to adopt a follow-the-leader mentality. But maybe, somewhere inside of you, you feel the desire to make things happen, to be the head, not the tail.

Then maybe, leadership just suits you fine. Some people believe that great leaders are made, not born. Yes, it may be true that some people are born with natural talents, however, without practice, drive, enthusiasm, and experience, there can be no true development in leadership. You must also remember that good leaders are continually working and studying to improve their natural skills.

# How to Reach Your Full Potential Every Day and Succeed

Why does it seem like time goes by so quickly? We start a week and before we know it, it's already the weekend. How can you make the best out of each day? When it comes to reaching your full potential every day, it's all about planning. If you're not a good planner, you'll have to start learning! Those who are good with time management and are organized, usually experience a more productive day. So, how do you reach your full potential?

### Having A Growth Mindset

A growth mindset believes anything is possible, but don't confuse this with being delusional! It's more of the way you think about and approach problems. Let's say you have an issue of not being good at public speaking. You with a growth mindset, will analyze this condition and come up with solutions to make it better. You may take a class on public speaking. Whatever it is, a growth mindset doesn't look at failure as a roadblock, but rather as a minor detour on the road to your destination.

## Focus on the Bigger Picture

What does the big picture look like to you? What are the goals that you want to accomplish? When it comes to reaching your potential every day, it's important that you know what the big picture looks like. Why do you do what you do? What is the reason that you go to work or come home and provide dinner for your family? When you have purpose and reason in your life, you're more able to live out each day to your fullest potential. If you can see the big picture in your life, you don't have to just live day-to-day. When you know your purpose, you will be motivated to live each day to your fullest potential.

# HOW TO FIND PURPOSE IN LIFE?

**Time Management:** Reaching your full potential every day is about planning your day in alignment with what matters to you.

**Focus on What is Important in Your Life:** Maybe it's providing for your family or spending quality time with your spouse. When you can live in alignment with what matters to you, you will be able to reach your fullest potential every day.

**Plan Weekly:** That way, you'll be able to see your week's schedule before starting your week. Make sure to add when you plan to start working and end working into your schedule. You need to know when it's time to turn off work mode and start spending quality time with your family. It's also important that when you plan your week, you are realistic about what you want to accomplish.

**Set Yourself Up for Success, Not for Failure:** Create a to-do list for each day of the week. Have about 4-5 tasks that you want to accomplish each day. If you have a big project, you should only include 2-3 tasks for that day. Planning and having good time management is a combination that contributes to reaching your fullest potential daily. Having good time management is important for you to learn because when you value yourself, you will value how you spend your time.

## TIPS TO MAXIMIZE YOUR PRODUCTIVITY

### Avoid Distractions

With so many distractions, it's easy to get off track and not get anything done. That's why staying focused on what you need to get done is key to reaching your fullest potential. If you get distracted by your phone, make sure you put it on silent when you're trying to finish a task. Not only will get a lot more done, but you will also prevent yourself from negatively affecting your well-being. Anything that distracts you from completing a task needs to be put away. The bottom line here is that while you may want to stop working at 5 pm sharp or watch the game on Saturday, developing the discipline to delay satisfaction will help push your boundaries and reap the rewards that come from that extra effort.

### Have a Positive Attitude

When it comes to reaching your fullest potential every day, it's important to have a positive attitude. When you have a negative attitude, you start viewing yourself and your life as being negative. How can you possibly reach your fullest potential when you have a negative attitude about yourself? It's all about your perspective and how you view yourself and your potential. To have a productive day, you must have a positive attitude to be able to stay focused on what you want to accomplish every day.

## Accept That You Will Fail

There is no such thing as an overnight success. Failure is a part of life and it happens to everyone. There is a whole body of thinking that failure is better than success. While most of us would agree that success is better than failure when it does happen, here is something to keep in mind: Don't take it personally. A failure in a job, career, business, or marriage is just that. It is not a reflection of you as a person. I had a friend who lost a fortune in a business deal. I called him shortly after and as expected he was very depressed. My only advice to him was: "Never confuse your self-worth with your net worth." Move on, failures can be heartbreaking, embarrassing, and demoralizing. Take the time needed to go through those feelings and process the emotions. Remember that your goal is to live up to your full potential and succeed in life. Dwelling on past mistakes and failures is the surest way to derail your progress.

## Embrace Simplicity

When you want to reach your fullest potential, simplify what needs to be done before the day starts. An easy place to start is with your morning routine. If you can find different ways to save time and make your life simpler, you'll be able to focus on reaching your fullest potential every day. When you are constantly all over the place and your life is far from being simple, you'll experience stress and frustration daily. Simplify your life!

## Recharge

You can only reach your fullest potential if you take the time to recharge. When you are constantly working without any rest, you will eventually burn out. It is not only important for you to recharge your mind– your body needs time to recharge too. Schedule downtime for yourself and use different strategies that help you relax. Reaching your fullest potential every day can become stressful if you don't manage your time well and take the time to recharge. Take a moment and think about what recharges you. Maybe it's spending some quality time with your spouse or taking a nice walk in the park. Whatever you decide to do, make sure you enjoy the process. It's easy for our minds to wander, so when you're recharging, focus on recharging!

## Enjoy Each Moment

"To get all there is out of living, we must employ our time wisely, never being in too much of a hurry to stop and sip life, but never losing our sense of the enormous value of a minute" –Robert Updegraff. With so much going on, it's easy to just go, go, go, and not take the time to smell the flowers. Enjoy the moments that you experience throughout each day. This will help you feel grateful and appreciative of what you have in your life. Enjoy the simple things like having a roof over your head and being able to afford food for your family.

## Practice Self-Discipline

Self-discipline is essentially your consistent ability to control your actions, feelings, and emotions. When it comes to your finances, you can stick to your plans of paying down debt, saving, and investing. Once you learn how to master self-discipline behaviors, you'll stay motivated and are more likely to achieve success. So it's strongly connected to willpower, which is the control of one's impulses and actions. Willpower is how you stay focused on a task, while self-discipline is more about when you take consistent action in advance to strengthen willpower. Both self-discipline and willpower go hand in hand.

## Live a More Balanced Life

How do you stay balanced in life? Is balance something truly achievable – or just a myth? We know too well what life out of balance feels like – stressful, overwhelming, exhausting. Even the smallest tasks seem daunting. But balance isn't something you simply are born with. It's something you work constantly at creating. By focusing on improving your mental, physical, and spiritual wellness and by making very intentional life changes, you can stay balanced in life, going from drained and maxed out to energized and capable of anything.

## Spend Time with the Right People

The relationships we have in our lives considerably affect our mental and physical health. Loving, supportive relationships not only protect against depression, but they can lower our blood pressure and even help us live longer. That's why it's important to nurture good relationships, surrounding yourself with people who make you feel good.

Just like other toxins in our environments, toxic people can have the same effect on your well-being. These individuals take more than they give, leaving you exhausted and overwhelmed. While they can be charismatic, which draws you in, they are also extremely negative – and manipulative. They suck the life out of the room; the world revolves around them.

Do you have an energy vampire in your life? You very likely do. Energy vampires are people who — sometimes intentionally — drain your emotional energy. They feed on your kindness, desire to care for them, and willingness to be there, leaving you feeling stressed out and empty. Identify these people and begin the process of eliminating them from your life. Replace them with people who strengthen and bolster you, add beautiful balance to your life, and inspire you to be a better version of yourself.

In some cases, that simply isn't possible. Sometimes energy vampires are co-workers, family members, or other individuals you haven't chosen as friends; you can't eliminate them from your life. Instead, you'll need to distance yourself from them, create healthy boundaries, and protect yourself from their negative energies.

## Establish Boundaries, and Learn to Say No

With all of life's challenges, we find ourselves pressured to say yes too often. Conflict is difficult, and many of us are people pleasers. Sometimes it is easier to say yes than deal with the fallout of "no". But, if you don't learn to say "no", your time – and your level of stress – cannot be controlled. Before saying yes, take a pause and consider what you already have on your plate. Think about what is reasonable – and what you can do. Reduce stress by learning how to say "no." It may be hard at first – but trust me, it gets easier every time you say it. And the number of asks decreased as well. Respect yourself, your time, and your balance in life – others will do the same.

## Give Yourself Time to Do Nothing

New research finds that giving ourselves time to do nothing improves our mental health, balance, and creativity. Our brains are filled with the task at hand, so often they have to ignore a stream of spontaneous thoughts, memories, and emotions. But there is growing research that this stream, known as your brain's default mode network, is good for us! Ever heard of being in the flow? Who would have thought the flow state starts when you are giving yourself the freedom to just be?

Our fast-paced culture values accomplishments and being busy – but being in this state is draining and can cause you to miss out on the benefits that mental downtime can offer. So go ahead – take a moment to pause, lose yourself in a daydream, and let your mind wander. In the end, you'll be more effective – and inspired.

## Find Balance by Focusing Within

To achieve mental and physical balance, you also need to focus on your spiritual self. Practicing meditation daily is an effective way to do this. Meditation enables you to deeply relax, become still, and calm your mind. While meditating, you focus on one thing, getting rid of the constant stream of busy thoughts that overrun your mind and cause stress. There's no denying meditation results in both physical and mental benefits. Meditation can improve sleep, reduce stress and anxiety, increase immunity, improve focus and memory, and create feelings of balance as well as compassion.

## Live in the Moment

In our busy world, many of us are living in the future. We are always creating lists and worrying about things we cannot control. There is always a long list of things we need to do, haven't managed to find time to accomplish, or feel we should do. These lists are ever-growing causing us to focus more time on the future – not the present. By avoiding obsessing about the future – and the "what ifs" – you can focus on the right now – what is happening today.

The key to balance is being present – with your family, friends, work, life and mind. Let go of the need to be in control of things you can't control. The future is tomorrow. The present is right now and is the only thing you can affect. If you find yourself constantly fast-forwarding to the future and worrying, a good hack is to ground yourself. Tune into what you are experiencing at this exact moment. What are you smelling, tasting, hearing, and seeing?

## Limit Technology, and Its Effects

There's no escaping it. Technology rules our lives. That's why it's important to ensure you are managing your technology – and not letting it manage you. Take time to reflect on what aspects of technology decrease and increase your stress. Then identify ways to take a technology time out. We've set timers on our scrolling and make a point to leave tech behind when we get into nature.

Excessive screen time has been shown to significantly affect you both mentally and physically – by impacting your sleep quality, increasing blood pressure, leading to insulin resistance, and obesity, causing poor stress regulation, leading to developmental issues in children, and causing feelings of isolation as well as anti-social behaviour. While there is a lot of conflicting information out there, we believe it's best to limit your technology reliance – getting your relationship with technology in balance to reduce stress.

## Find Balance Naturally

Balance starts with what we put into – and do – with our bodies. Eating in a balanced, intentional manner that is healthy is critical to reducing stress and improving our health. Eat organically, consume whole foods like plenty of fruits and vegetables, cut out the caffeine, sugar, processed foods, and alcohol, and consciously feed your mind, body, and soul.

Do you ever find yourself feeling exhausted or overwhelmed? Most people are busy with family, work, hobbies, or community responsibilities. Sometimes people allow their schedules to take control of their lives, and priorities might get disorganized. As a result, they may feel stressed, frustrated, and tired. When your life is feeling a little imbalanced, it may feel as though you have neglected your needs, values, or priorities. Although it may be easy to feel regretful and burned out at that moment, you can still work toward achieving a sense of equilibrium.

*The following practices will help bring balance back into your life:*

**Be reasonable**. People have a limit on resources like time, money, and energy. It is completely understandable to want to accomplish many things; however, it is important to consider how much time is in a day. Know that you are one person. Erase the idea of perfection and problem-solving for others—it's okay not to get everything done. You are doing your best.

**Find a support system**. Find the people in your life who build you up and support you, who add value to your life, and inspire you to be a better version of yourself. Try to avoid people who add or create more stress for you. Remember that stress will affect you physically, so, within reason, consider phasing out those who might be causing your stress or imbalance.

**Take control and say no**. People often say yes to others because they may feel an unreasonable pressure to immediately please people. It is important to consider your current list of responsibilities and take time to think about what you can reasonably complete. Try to alleviate adding extra stress by learning how to say no.

**Make a schedule for rest**. Resting doesn't always have to mean sleeping, it can mean, reading, listening to music or a podcast, or utilizing a creative outlet. Whatever you choose, do things that bring you comfort and peace.

**Focus on today**. There will always be something that we will need to do, haven't gotten to, or something we have always wanted to do.

Try to avoid obsessing about the future and focus on what is happening today. Creating a healthy, balanced life requires you to be present in your family, friends, hobbies, and work. Remember, there is more to life than the daily stressors that create imbalance and unhappiness. Start taking steps toward a more balanced life by learning how to take control, set boundaries, and focus on today.

# STAND UP AND PUSH

*Motsamai*
*Keep Going*

When you are alone and busy thinking of the direction your life is taking, you start to wonder a lot when you see no positive results in the efforts you put into your plans. No one understands the weight of your trials towards success but I for one, can relate to your storyline. I worked in the hospitality industry and I disliked every moment I spent in that industry as it brought only discontentment. I was a person of no value without appropriate formal education or training.

I had to take odd jobs to meet basic needs and working in hotels was one of those odd jobs. I had to work to survive. I performed my duties in exchange for money, not that I valued my job. Daily I would make affirmations that this job is not meant for me and I had to move on to pursue my childhood dreams. I would often see people of a younger generation accumulating basic needs, wealth, and being formally educated whereas I remained below the average line.

My life was chaotic. I lived almost a decade with undiagnosed depression for having a wrong focus. You might have tried to improve your life and along the way, you were forced, or rather let me say, you chose to give up. Did you see yourself as a failure then? Well, the saddest truth is that there is no failure except when you stop pursuing your goals through and beyond limitations. You see when you quit on something, it's an indication to you that somewhere out there, there is something better than what you are giving up on. Dreams that you had when you just graduated from the university, fade away because of irrational limitations you created in your mind. Disappointments and setbacks are part and parcel of the process of any individual's transformation and empowerment.

Perhaps you didn't know how to challenge the limitations you are facing or faced then. Whatever the reason you fabricated for losing hope and settling for less, giving up on your goals, your mindset is the only element that misled you to have such faulty beliefs. Whatever you put your mind to it grows, either positively or negatively. So, be careful what you entertain in your daily thoughts.

### Do the Hustle

There's a certain urgency to success that doesn't apply so much to the fruits of success as it does to the desire for success. You have to want to succeed before you can even begin to try to succeed. You have to want success more than you want anything else. It is this desire that activates the work ethic that's necessary to succeed. That's right, there is a definite work ethic that successful people bring to the table. If you want to succeed, then you have to emulate this work ethic. You have to want to succeed so much that you hustle. Hustling is all about walking the success walk. Anyone can talk about success. As they say, talk is cheap. You can talk about success all day long and not get one step closer to actually being successful. The only way to reach your goals is to put in the work necessary. This work requires concentration, creativity, and conscious effort. There's no secret here. You're going to have to sweat to get there. The hours are long and the tasks are consuming. There's no such thing as instant success or overnight success. Often the people who appear to be enjoying overnight success have hustled hard for months and years to get that success. So, remember that success means work, and work means to hustle. Go the extra mile in everything you do. In the long run, those extra miles will put you ahead of the pack, and much closer to where you want to be.

Tell me, how bad are you willing to suffer for your success? I ask this question because you cannot plan to achieve greater things and expect to sail through without obstacles. Otherwise, everyone would have been successful in nature if the road to success was paved without limitations. The need to gain power and succeed is an inner motivation that is reliant on your self-worth. How much do you value yourself? As for me, I value myself beyond limits and I will keep pushing until I see something positive happening.

If you believe that you are meant for greater things in life, definitely you shall earn your prize. I say earn not deserve because reaching success involves hard and smart work. You need to earn success as a reward for the efforts you have invested in your daily activities. You need to stand up and fight for success. It will not be handed over to you on a silver platter but through hard work, consistency, and staying focused all the time. As much as life is a journey, so is success. For you to grasp what is yours, you need to prepare adequately within your purpose. By pushing beyond your limits, you can become everything that you ever wanted to be. You can achieve your dreams and leave a lasting legacy. *The tips below can help you to achieve that, and I recommend that you apply them in your life to see a gradual, positive personal transformation and empowerment.*

## Push Yourself Beyond Limits

Everyone has dreams and goals. However, very few people achieve them. This is because the majority of us let our limitations hold us back. These limitations take various forms. Examples are physical inability, doubt, fear, or a negative past. When you meet your limits, you feel resistance and ultimately stagnation. This makes everything feel much harder to accomplish. Many people around the world are unable to hold on when it gets to this point. Therefore, they give up. It is important to learn how to beat your limits and overcome them. This enables you to achieve your goals.

## Find Someone to Assist You

Sometimes all that you need to overcome your limitations and keep moving towards your dreams is a little encouragement. It is important to have someone to support you when things get tough. They can be a counter-balance for any negative thinking or self-talk that you could have when the going gets hard. By showing you how strong you are, they can help you to shift focus from your limitations to your strengths. As a result, you can accomplish more and push yourself to do the things that exist beyond your comfort zone. This is a sure way to achieve your big dream.

## Embrace Bigger Challenges

The fundamental activity required in pushing beyond your limits is to take on challenges that are harder than what you are used to. If you do not push past your capability regularly, you get stuck within your comfort zone and do not experience any growth. This causes stagnation and eventually despair. Therefore, enthusiastically embrace challenges that are bigger, harder, and more complex than what you are used to. This will help you to get comfortable being outside your comfort zone and get you closer to your dreams.

## Go For What Is Unknown To You

The majority of us are afraid of the unknown. We feel threatened when we even think of going past our comfort zones. This shows a low ability to handle ambiguity. When there is an unknown chance of success or failure, we are afraid to move forward. Research shows that children are more willing to embrace the unknown than adults. This is because the desire for safety and security is much stronger as we grow older. This makes us want to stay within our comfort zone more.

However, the only way to overcome our limits is to embrace the unknown. Moreover, if you currently enjoy and are satisfied with your current work, you will be able to embrace the discomfort that comes with the unknown. According to Bill Walsh, who is the San Francisco 49ers' former head coach, "if your reason why is bold enough, then you will know how to get where you want to be."

## Visualize Yourself at the Next Level

One of the most important activities to perform to push past your limits is to stay focused. Visualization is a handy tool that you can use to this effect. You need to focus on what you want to get motivated in pursuing your plan despite your imagined limits. Many times, we know where we have been and where we currently are. However, we rarely know exactly where we need to go. Take the time to imagine where you want to be by a certain time in the future. Visualize this every single morning when you get up. This will motivate you to go out of your comfort zone and pursue your goals.

# REDISCOVER YOUR LIFE!

*Motsamai*
*Keep Going*

Just so that you don't make a big blunder in life again, it is important to understand that, success does not always mean being the best and achieving the most. Everyday things that we don't consider important are a part of our success in life. To know and identify if you are being revitalized, you will recognize these particular aspects:

- There is no room for drama in maturity. If your relationships were full of drama in the past, but now you have put that behind you, it is a clear sign of success. Asking for help is a sign of strength, not weakness. Success is impossible if you isolate yourself from other people. You can accomplish your goals only if you work in a team and asking for help means you have grown a lot as a person.

- You won't tolerate bad behaviour, no matter who it comes from. Everyone is responsible for their actions and you know it. You let go things that don't make you feel good. It sounds narcissistic; however, it is a sign that you love yourself enough to let go of the things you feel uncomfortable with.

- You should appreciate what you see in the mirror at any given moment of the day. If you are always aware of how much you are worth, it means you have succeeded in life. No one is 100% successful, and no one is perfect. In life, you will encounter victories and losses and the latter should be your setting stone for something much better.

- Don't look at your losses as setbacks, instead consider them a thing that makes you grow into a stronger person. If you are well aware of the people who will always stand up for you and pick you up when you are at the bottom, you are a very successful person. This lesson is learned the hard way because, to see who is there for you, you will be betrayed many times in life.

- You are aware that complaining about things no matter how horrible they were will never change anything. You know that you should live here and now and you are grateful for the life you were given. If others succeed it does not mean you have failed. Praise those who are rising and giving positive energy towards them will only result in that positive energy returning to you.

- You never sit in the same place because you are aware that you can contribute to the world with your unique talents and gifts. You are not just aware of it; in fact, you take action. You constantly need things in your life that you will anticipate eagerly unless you will be slowly dying.

+ You need to create your goals and let the excitement of working towards them lead you to your success. Failures and losses are an inevitable part of life, however, sticking to your goals will result in success, most of the time. Experiencing victory will give you the energy boost to keep going and create new goals.

+ Being empathetic means you can spread love and positivity wherever you go. Successful people love other people just like they love their family members. You love deeply and open yourself up to be loved by others. Love carries its risks, and it is scary for some people because of the possibility of being rejected.

+ Being able to open your heart without the fear of the outcome means you have succeeded and grown as a person. You are the creator of your life experiences but these experiences are often given to you without your consent. This is why you need to be strong and accept them without being let down. You don't care what other people think. So, instead, you are true to yourself and love yourself just the way you are. You always look on the bright side.

+ Life is often filled with disappointments but only if you choose to look at them that way. Disappointments can also be viewed as learning opportunities and if you choose to learn from them, they are no longer negative experiences.

- You can't have full control over every aspect of your life. However, you have control over how you feel about the things that happen to you.

If you can look at things from the positive side, you are a successful person. You change the things you can. There are more things you can change in your life than you may think. Just remember that successful people never accept the negative things that can be changed. So, if there is something that bothers you, stand up and do something about it. *Keep Going!*

# A Life Plan Template

*Motsamai*
*Keep Going*

We all have hopes, dreams, and aspirations in life. But how many of us actually achieve our goals? Often we spend a lot of time thinking or talking about what we want. But we don't take steps to achieve it. It's not because we're lazy. It's because we don't know where to start. Therefore, as discussed previously, Use this step-by-step guide life planning template to help you get started.

## Why Must You Have a Life Plan

- A life plan helps you make your dreams a reality. A life plan gives you the confidence to take action and overcome your fears.
- A life plan helps you prioritize. Making a life plan helps you identify your priorities. This way, you only focus on things that move you in the direction of your dreams.
- A life plan helps you make better decisions. Knowing your goals and values can guide your decision-making process. This helps you make decisions that are in line with them.
- A life plan keeps you motivated. Writing down your goals is essential for staying focused on them. Place your life plan somewhere you can see it and read it every day to stay motivated.

- A life plan makes you feel empowered. A life plan gives you a sense of control over your destiny. It reminds you that the ability to achieve your dreams is in your hands.

# A LIFE PLAN: A STEP-BY-STEP GUIDE

*Follow This Process To Create Your Life Plan:*

### Create a Vision

To get started, imagine your dream life. Be as specific in the details as possible. Picture yourself already there and write out your vision. Once you have written your vision, think about what you need to do to achieve it. Make a list of steps, such as gaining a new certification or reaching a certain income level. Try to be realistic, but at the same time, don't hold yourself back from dreaming big.

..............................................................................................................................

..............................................................................................................................

..............................................................................................................................

..............................................................................................................................

..............................................................................................................................

..............................................................................................................................

..............................................................................................................................

..............................................................................................................................

..............................................................................................................................

..............................................................................................................................

..............................................................................................................................

..............................................................................................................................

## Perform a Self-Assessment

A self-assessment of your achievements so far gives you a starting point for your life plan. Take stock of your successes as well as your failures. Look for the lessons learned and experiences you don't want to repeat. Identify your strengths and weaknesses. When doing your self-assessment, look at different areas of your life, including:

- Relationships
- Personal growth
- Finances
- Health

Grade each area on a satisfaction level of one to five. This will help you identify your strengths as well as your areas for improvement.

..................................................................................................................
..................................................................................................................
..................................................................................................................
..................................................................................................................
..................................................................................................................
..................................................................................................................
..................................................................................................................
..................................................................................................................
..................................................................................................................
..................................................................................................................
..................................................................................................................
..................................................................................................................
..................................................................................................................

## Prioritize Your Life

Now that you have your vision and areas for growth, it's time to prioritize. You don't need to set detailed goals at this stage. The aim of this step is to decide what's essential and what you need to let go off. Your time is precious, so you need to invest it wisely. Prioritizing will help you do so.

..................................................................................................................
..................................................................................................................
..................................................................................................................
..................................................................................................................
..................................................................................................................
..................................................................................................................
..................................................................................................................
..................................................................................................................
..................................................................................................................
..................................................................................................................
..................................................................................................................
..................................................................................................................
..................................................................................................................
..................................................................................................................

## Identify Your Values

Analyzing your past can help you identify your values. When you look back at past decisions, you can see what the motivating factors were behind them. For example, if your career trajectory has been one in which your income has steadily grown over time, it shows that money is one of your core values. But if you've chosen fewer responsibilities at work in exchange for less money, it means you probably value less stress and more free time. Negative past experiences also teach us about our values. They show us the things we want to avoid experiencing again. Bearing your values in mind will help you make decisions that are in line with your dreams.

.......................................................................................................................
.......................................................................................................................
.......................................................................................................................
.......................................................................................................................
.......................................................................................................................
.......................................................................................................................
.......................................................................................................................
.......................................................................................................................
.......................................................................................................................
.......................................................................................................................
.......................................................................................................................
.......................................................................................................................
.......................................................................................................................

## Establish SMART Goals

Once you've identified your vision and take stock of your priorities and values, the next step is to set effective goals. Aim to set both medium and long-term goals that are realistic and achievable. Identify different goals for the areas of your life you evaluated in your self-assessment. Make sure they align with your priorities and values.

*Use the SMART method to set effective goals.*

...................................................................................................................
...................................................................................................................
...................................................................................................................
...................................................................................................................
...................................................................................................................
...................................................................................................................
...................................................................................................................
...................................................................................................................
...................................................................................................................
...................................................................................................................
...................................................................................................................
...................................................................................................................
...................................................................................................................
...................................................................................................................
...................................................................................................................
...................................................................................................................

### Outline an Action Plan

Your action plan should detail a step-by-step process that will help you work toward your intermediate goals. Identify the daily actions that will add up over time and help you build momentum. Schedule them in your calendar and commit to taking action every day. Place your action plan somewhere you will see it —

for example, above your desk. Don't forget to celebrate every milestone and reward yourself for your achievements.

........................................................................................................
........................................................................................................
........................................................................................................
........................................................................................................
........................................................................................................
........................................................................................................
........................................................................................................
........................................................................................................
........................................................................................................
........................................................................................................
........................................................................................................
........................................................................................................
........................................................................................................
........................................................................................................
........................................................................................................
........................................................................................................
........................................................................................................

## Adjust As Necessary

Remember, your life plan is a tool that guides you toward your goals. However, we all experience setbacks at some point, and that's okay. If you miss a goal or take longer than planned to reach it, don't give up. Revise your life plan and make adjustments as needed.

# The Right Questions to Ask When Making a Life Plan

*As you write your life plan, ask yourself the following questions, and keep your answers in mind:*

## What Results Do You Want To Achieve?

As you create the vision of your dream life, try to be as specific as possible. Think about the results that accompany your desired outcome. For example, let's say your goal is to become a director in your company. Ask yourself why you want to achieve this goal, and what difference it would make in your life.

........................................................................................................................

........................................................................................................................

........................................................................................................................

........................................................................................................................

........................................................................................................................

........................................................................................................................

........................................................................................................................

........................................................................................................................

........................................................................................................................

........................................................................................................................

........................................................................................................................

........................................................................................................................

........................................................................................................................

........................................................................................................................

## What Actions Will Achieve Those Results?

Once you know the results, work backward to define the steps that will help you make continuous progress toward that objective. Make sure you identify any actions that might require support. Make a list of trusted friends and loved ones and ask them to help you.

.................................................................................................................
.................................................................................................................
.................................................................................................................
.................................................................................................................
.................................................................................................................
.................................................................................................................
.................................................................................................................
.................................................................................................................
.................................................................................................................
.................................................................................................................
.................................................................................................................
.................................................................................................................

## How Will You Stay Motivated?

Writing a life plan can be fun and exciting. It can also increase your motivation levels. But one day soon, something may happen that deflates your motivation like an old balloon. Maybe you'll come up against an unforeseen challenge. Perhaps you'll fall out with your best friend. Or maybe you'll just get out of the wrong side of the bed. Whatever it is, you'll lose your motivation. You'll want to throw in the towel. And that's why you need to prepare by asking yourself how you will stay motivated. When you're working toward a big goal, break it down into smaller goals. Celebrate and reward yourself for those achievements. Ask your trusted friends and loved ones to help you stay motivated when the going gets rough.

........................................................................................................................
........................................................................................................................
........................................................................................................................
........................................................................................................................
........................................................................................................................
........................................................................................................................
........................................................................................................................
........................................................................................................................
........................................................................................................................
........................................................................................................................
........................................................................................................................
........................................................................................................................
........................................................................................................................
........................................................................................................................
........................................................................................................................

## How Will You Measure Progress?

Setting milestone goals is a good way to measure your progress. The best way to measure progress would be to break it down into smaller goals. These goals might include developing new skills. This will help make sure you implement your life plan within the specified time frame.

.............................................................................................
.............................................................................................
.............................................................................................
.............................................................................................
.............................................................................................
.............................................................................................
.............................................................................................
.............................................................................................
.............................................................................................
.............................................................................................
.............................................................................................
.............................................................................................
.............................................................................................
.............................................................................................

## Areas To Also Include in Your Life Plan

Some people want to plan every aspect of their lives. You might decide to plan in some areas, but not in others. It's your life plan, so it's up to you what to include. To inspire you more, here are five of the most common areas to include in your life plan:

### Health And Well-Being

Health is true wealth. Without it, nothing else matters. Whether you're healthy, unhealthy, or somewhere in between, health and well-being should be on your life plan. Even if you're fit and healthy now, it's always wise to plan ahead — your future self will thank you for it.

........................................................................................
........................................................................................
........................................................................................
........................................................................................
........................................................................................
........................................................................................
........................................................................................
........................................................................................
........................................................................................
........................................................................................
........................................................................................
........................................................................................
........................................................................................

## Relationships

Whether you're single or in a committed partnership, there are always ways to improve your relationships. All relationships start with the relationship you have with yourself. If you're bitter or self-loathing, those qualities can influence your relationships. Beyond that, there are ways to learn to be a better partner, friend, parent, or relative. Perhaps you want to be a better listener. Maybe you want to be more patient with your kids. Or maybe you yearn for a deeper connection with your partner.

........................................................................................
........................................................................................
........................................................................................
........................................................................................
........................................................................................
........................................................................................

..................................................................................................................
..................................................................................................................
..................................................................................................................
..................................................................................................................
..................................................................................................................
..................................................................................................................
..................................................................................................................

## Career

If you're unhappy with your current job, you need a plan to change it. But even if you're happy with where you are now, you still need to plan for your future growth and development. And if you're an entrepreneur, you already know planning is a prerequisite for business success.

..................................................................................................................
..................................................................................................................
..................................................................................................................
..................................................................................................................
..................................................................................................................
..................................................................................................................
..................................................................................................................
..................................................................................................................
..................................................................................................................
..................................................................................................................
..................................................................................................................
..................................................................................................................
..................................................................................................................
..................................................................................................................

## Finances

Financial planning is closely linked to your career aspirations. Set realistic financial goals according to the profession you choose. When setting financial goals, think about your priorities and values. For example, if spending time with your family is important to you, you might decide to prioritize more free time over more money. If that's the case, you might not want to aim for the role of CEO. Therefore, you won't aim for a CEO's salary, either. Adjust your financial goals accordingly.

...............................................................................................................
...............................................................................................................
...............................................................................................................
...............................................................................................................
...............................................................................................................
...............................................................................................................
...............................................................................................................
...............................................................................................................
...............................................................................................................

## Community

One of the secrets to a long and healthy life is to be part of a community. According to research, loneliness is as bad for your health as smoking. Ways to include it in your life plan:

- Schedule regular get-togethers with friends and family.
- Volunteer in your community, such as at a care home.
- Participate in religious or spiritual groups.

..................................................................................................
..................................................................................................
..................................................................................................
..................................................................................................
..................................................................................................
..................................................................................................
..................................................................................................
..................................................................................................

**A Life Plan** is a guide that helps move you toward your goals. It should be flexible enough to adapt when something isn't working. If you struggle to meet your goals, work with your life coach to adjust your life plan and set more realistic goals.

# Make it Happen!!!

*Motsamai*
*Keep Going*